THE LION'S SHARE

د زمري برخه

English Animal Idioms

(Pashto - English)

د ځناورو په اړه انګليسي محاورې

(پښتو- انګليسي)

By Troon Harrison
Illustrated by Dmitry Fedorov
Pashto translation by Tariq Kamal

Language Lizard
Basking Ridge

For English audio and resources for teaching idioms, see the last page of this book.

Published by Language Lizard
Basking Ridge, NJ 07920
info@LanguageLizard.com

Visit us at www.LanguageLizard.com

LCCN: 2020904810 (English)

ISBN: 978-1-63685-517-2 (Print)

WHAT IS AN IDIOM?

An idiom is a phrase that says one thing but means something different. An idiom can be a quick way of saying something complicated. Knowing idioms will help you to understand and speak English fluently. This book contains idioms about animals. *Note - The English idioms are translated* ***literally.***

محاوره څه ته وائي؟

محاوره هغه جملې ته وئيلې شي کومه چې په وينه کې يو شان وي ولې مطلب ئي بل څه وي. کيدې شي يوه محاوره د يو ګراني خبرې کولو آسانه لار وي. د محاورو پيژندل به تاسو سره مرسته وکړي چې په انګليسي ژبه پوه شئ او خبرې وکړئ. دا کتاب د ځناورو په اړه محاورې لري.

يادونه - دا انګليسي محاورې په **لفظي** توګه ژباړل شوي.

ANTS IN YOUR PANTS

ستاسو پتلون كي ميګي

Meaning: Not being able to stay still

معني: په يو ځائي نه شي ټينګيدلي

I can tell you are excited to see your grandmother because you have **ants in your pants.**

GETS MY GOAT

زما بيزه قبضه کوي

Meaning: Feeling annoyed

معني: په چا غصه کيدل

It really **gets my goat** when my sister eats all the snacks.

BUSY AS A BEE

د مچۍ په ثیر بوخت

Meaning: To work hard and quickly at a job

معني: په یو کار کې په چټکۍ او سختۍ سره کار کول

When Mom cleans the house, she is **busy as a bee**.

RAINING CATS AND DOGS

د پیشوګانو او سپیو باران

Meaning: Heavy rain that makes you very wet

معني: ډیر زیات باران چې بنده ډیر زیات لوندوي

I forgot to bring my umbrella and now it is raining cats and dogs.

HOLD YOUR HORSES

خپل آسونه قابو کړئ

Meaning: Be patient and don't be hasty

معني: صبر وکړه او بيړه مه کوه

Hold your horses! You can join your friends after you finish your chores.

GET MY DUCKS IN A ROW

زما بطخي قطار كي ولاړي دي

Meaning: To be well prepared for something that is going to happen

معني: د هغه څه لپاره ښه چمتو کيدل چې مخي ته راتلو والا وي

Before moving to another country,
I had to **get my ducks in a row**.

BUTTERFLIES IN MY STOMACH

په معده کي د جنت مرغي

Meaning: Feeling nervous or excited

معني: د اضطراب او جوش احساس کول

When I sing on stage, I get **butterflies in my stomach**.

TAKE THE BULL BY THE HORNS

غوائي د ښکرو نه راټينګول

Meaning: Being brave, facing up to a challenge

معني: نرتوب، له ننګونو سره مخ کېدل

I was scared to compete, but my coach told me to **take the bull by the horns**.

AS THE CROW FLIES
لکه څنګه چې کارغه پرواز کوي

Meaning: The straight, direct route

معني: نیغه، مستقیمه لار

The man thought it was not far to the valley **as the crow flies**.

UNTIL THE COWS COME HOME

تر هغه وخت پورې چې غواګانې کور ته نه وي راغلي

Meaning: Doing something for a very long time

معني: د ډېر وخت لپاره يو څه کار کول

There is so much to sweep, I'll be working **until the cows come home**.

AT A SNAIL'S PACE

د شاپیتۍ په رفتار

Meaning: Doing something very slowly

معني: یو کار ډېر رو رو کول

When I'm late for school, Mom says I am moving **at a snail's pace.**

SMELL A RAT
د منګک بوئ

Meaning: Feeling that something is wrong

معني: احساس کول چې يو څه غلط دی

A man said the bridge was safe, but I smelled a rat.

LET THE CAT OUT OF THE BAG

پرېږدئ چې پیشو له کڅوړې څخه راوځي

Meaning: Giving away a secret

معني: پټې خبرې ښکاره کول

I wanted the party to be a surprise, but I accidentally **let the cat out of the bag.**

THE LION'S SHARE

د زمري برخه

Meaning: Having the most of something

معني: په يو څه کي غټه برخه اغستل

I tried to cut the pizza in half, but Dad told me to take **the lion's share.**

Visit www.LanguageLizard.com/Animal-Idioms for additional resources for teaching and learning English idioms, including:

- English audio of this book
- Multicultural lesson plans for use in the classroom or at home
- Information on the origin of the idioms in this book
- Additional animal idioms with their meaning, usage, and origin
- Information on idiom translations and idioms in other languages

This book is part of the **Language Lizard Idiom Series**.

Visit **www.LanguageLizard.com** for a complete listing of the titles in this series and available languages.

www.ingramcontent.com/pod-product-compliance
Ingram Content Group UK Ltd.
Pitfield, Milton Keynes, MK11 3LW, UK
UKHW051125300826
14795UKWH00023B/700

9 781636 855172